This book belongs to:

____

Made in the USA
Middletown, DE
11 October 2023

40654451R00062